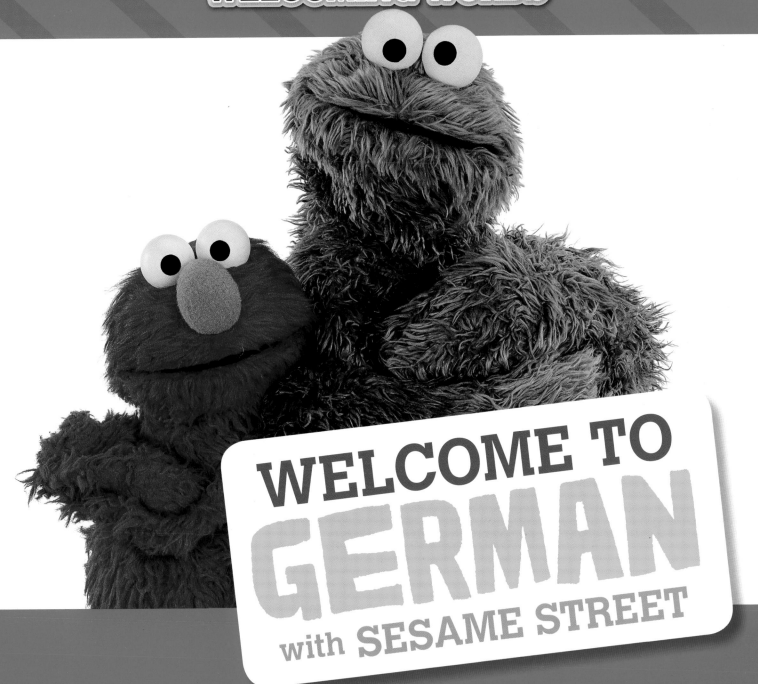

123 SESAME STREET

WELCOMING WORDS

WELCOME TO GERMAN

with SESAME STREET

J. P. PRESS

Lerner Publications ◆ Minneapolis

Dear Parents and Educators,

From its very beginning, *Sesame Street* has promoted mutual respect and cultural understanding by featuring a cast of diverse and lovable characters. *Welcome to German* introduces children to the wonderful, wide world we live in. In this book *Sesame Street* friends present handy and fun vocabulary in a language kids may not know. These words can help young readers welcome new friends. Have fun as you explore!

Sincerely,

The Editors at Sesame Workshop

Table of Contents

WELCOME!

Herzlich willkommen!

HERTZ-lih
VEEL-koh-men

4

How to Speak German!

Practice speaking German! Each word is broken up into separate sounds called syllables. Do you see the syllable in CAPITAL LETTERS? That's the sound that you emphasize the most!

Some words in German change a little for men and women. In this book we switch back and forth.

Hello.
Hallo.
HA-lo

This is Finchen.
He lives in Germany.

My name is . . .
Ich heiße . . .
eeh HEIS-uh . . .

7

friendship
freundschaft
FROIND-shahft

friend
freund
froind

**Will you be
my friend?**

**Willst du meine
Freundin sein?**

villst doo MY-nuh
FROIN-deen sine

Meet my family!
Lerne meine Familie kennen!
LAIR-nuh MY-nuh FAH-mih-lee KE-nen

dad
papa
PA-pa

mom
mama
MA-ma

brother
bruder
BROO-der

sister
schwester
SHVES-ter

grandma
oma
OH-ma

grandpa
opa
OH-pa

Thank you.
Danke.

You are welcome.
Bitte schön.
BIT-uh shoon

Please.
Bitte.
BIT-uh

I'm sorry.
Es tut mir leid.
es toot meer lide

13

lunch
mittagessen
mih-tag-ESS-en

breakfast
frühstück
FROO-schtuhk

snack
snack
snehck

dinner
abendessen
ahb-end-ESS-en

I'm thirsty.
Ich bin durstig.
eeh bin DUHR-schtick

hungry
hungrig
HUN-grick

How are you?
Wie geht es dir?
vee get es dihr

I'm fine, thank you.
Mir geht es gut, danke.
meer get es guht, DAWN-kuh

16

I like you.
Ich mag dich.
eeh mag dih

17

happy
glücklich
GLOOK-lih

sad
traurig
TROW-rig

proud
stolz
schtohltz

excited

aufgeregt
OWF-geh-rehgt

19

dog
hund
hoondt

animals
tiere
TIER-uh

fish
fisch
fish

cat
katze
KAT-zuh

hamster
hamster
HAHM-stair

I like animals.

Ich mag Tiere.

21

colors
farben
FAHR-ben

My favorite color is . . .
Meine
Lieblingsfarbe
ist . . .
MY-nuh LEEB-
lings-FAHR-
buh ist . . .

red
rot
roht

orange
orange
OH-rawnge

yellow
gelb
gelb

green
grün
groon

blue
blau
blauw

purple
lila
LEE-la

Let's play!
Lass uns spielen!
lahs oonz
SCHPEEL-en

toys
spielsachen
SCHPEEL-saw-hen

24

What do you like to do?
Was möchtest du gerne tun?
vahs MOH-test doo
GAIR-nuh toon

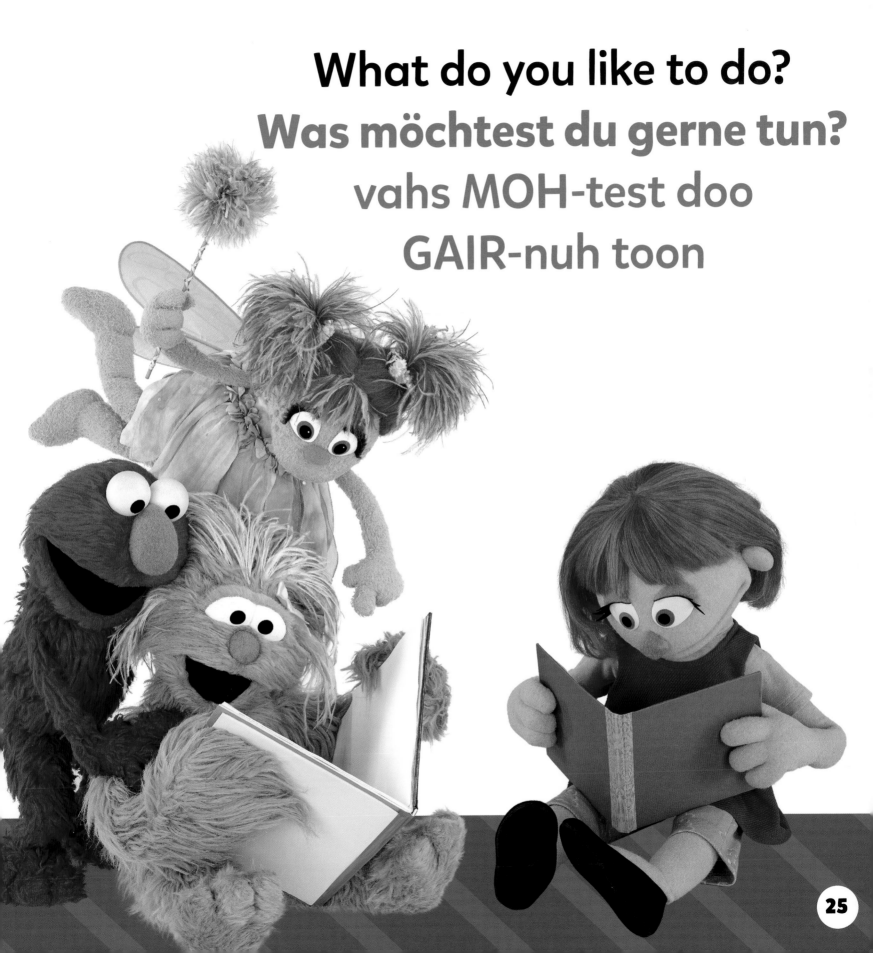

Goodbye.
Auf Wiedersehen.
owf VEE-der-sane

See you
soon!
Bis bald!

Count It!

1 one
eins
eintz

2 two
zwei
svy

3 three
drei
dry

4 four
vier
fear

7 seven
sieben
ZEE-ben

5 five
fünf
foonf

8 eight
acht
awkt

6 six
sechs
zex

9 nine
neun
noin

10 ten
zehn
tzen

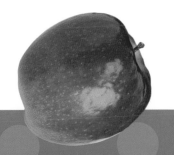

Bert and Ernie's Favorite Words

bubbles
schaum
shaum

bird
vogel
FOH-gull

stripes
streifen
SHTRIE-fen

It's bath time!
Zeit zum Baden!

Further Information

Billings, Patricia. *My First Bilingual Book—Sharing (English-German)*. Chicago: Milet, 2018.

Hello-World: German
http://www.hello-world.com/languages.php/?language=German&translate=English

National Geographic Kids: Germany
https://kids.nationalgeographic.com/explore/countries/germany/#germany-munich-city-scene.jpg

Sesame Street
http://www.sesamestreet.org

Tieck, Sarah. *Germany*. Minneapolis: Abdo, 2014.

Lerner Publications Company
An imprint of Lerner Publishing Group, Inc.
241 First Avenue North
Minneapolis, MN 55401 USA

For reading levels and more information, look up this title at www.lernerbooks.com.

Main body text set in Mikado.
Typeface provided by HVD.

Additional image credits: ESB Professional/Shutterstock.com, p. 20 (dog); Eric Isselee/Shutterstock.com, p. 20 (cat); Elya Vatel/Shutterstock.com, p. 20 (hamster); Gunnar Pippel/Shutterstock.com, p. 20 (fish); Super Prin/Shutterstock.com, p. 23 (butterfly).

Library of Congress Cataloging-in-Publication Data

Names: Press, J. P., 1993– author. | Children's Television Workshop, contributor.
Title: Welcome to German with Sesame Street / J. P. Press.
Other titles: Sesame Street (Television program)
Description: Minneapolis : Lerner Publications, 2019. | Series: Sesame Street welcoming words | Includes bibliographical references.
Identifiers: LCCN 2018059306 (print) | LCCN 2019007691 (ebook) | ISBN 9781541562493 (eb pdf) | ISBN 9781541554993 (lb : alk. paper) | ISBN 9781541574946 (pb : alk. paper)
Subjects: LCSH: German language—Conversation and phrasebooks—English—Juvenile literature.
Classification: LCC PF3121 (ebook) | LCC PF3121 .P84 2019 (print) | DDC 438.3/421—dc23

LC record available at https://lccn.loc.gov/2018059306

Manufactured in the United States of America
1-45823-42700-3/7/2019